W9-DBZ-133

Homeland Security Act of 2002, The : Leg

THE HOMELAND SECURITY ACT OF 2002

Legislation to Protect America

Steven P. Olson

The Rosen Publishing Group, Inc., New York

To babies Zachary and Willem, safe and secure at home

Published in 2006 by The Rosen Publishing Group, Inc.
29 East 21st Street, New York, NY 10010

First Edition

Library of Congress Cataloging-in-Publication Data

Olson, Steven P.
The Homeland Security Act of 2002: legislation to protect America/by Steven P. Olson.–1st ed.
    p. cm.–(The library of American laws and legal principles)
Includes bibliographical references.
ISBN 1-4042-0456-3 (library binding)
1. United States. Homeland Security Act of 2002. 2. United States. Dept. of Homeland Security. 3. National security–Law and legislation–United States. 4. Terrorism–United States–Prevention. I. Title. II. Series.
KF4651.O447 2006
343.73'01–dc22

                                                                    2005003621

Manufactured in the United States of America

On the cover: The main entrance of the United States Supreme Court building faces the U.S. Capitol in Washington, D.C. The marble statue on the right side of the entrance represents Authority of Law and was carved by James Earle Fraser. The male figure holds a sword and a tablet, on which is written the Latin word *Lex*, meaning "law."

CONTENTS

INTRODUCTION

Give me your tired, your poor,
Your huddled masses yearning to breathe free,
The wretched refuse of your teeming shore,
Send these, the homeless, tempest-tossed, to me:
I lift my lamp beside the golden door.

The inscription above is written on a plaque below the Statue of Liberty. It has welcomed millions of immigrants who came to the United States in search of freedom and opportunity. The United States represents a dream of great possibility for people in countries where suffering and poverty are common and civil rights are few. Those who have come to pursue their dreams have developed the United States into the most powerful nation on earth, where freedom and opportunity are treasured.

Yet, freedom is not free. Where freedoms exist, there must be laws to protect those freedoms and the people who enjoy them.

As early as 1875, the federal government placed limits on immigration. As the United States grew into an international power, more and more people wanted to move into the country. Consequently, more laws have been created to regulate immigration. Today, along the 1,945-mile (3,130-kilometer) border between the United States and Mexico, some of those laws have resulted in steel fences, helicopter patrols, and armed guards.

Immigrants wave American flags after being sworn in as American citizens at a mass ceremony at the Los Angeles Sports Arena in California on March 28, 2003. Each year, millions of immigrants pour into the United States, and hundreds of thousands become American citizens.

WARNING SIGNS

While most of the people who would like to enter the United States are seeking American freedoms, recent events have shown that some immigrants are coming to terrorize the American populace. On February 26, 1993, a bomb detonated in an underground parking garage at the World Trade Center in New York City, the same buildings that would later be destroyed in the September 11, 2001, attacks. Although the bomb failed to topple the building, six people died in the attack. Two years later, the personal computer of the mastermind behind the attack was found. It contained plans to attack eleven U.S. commercial airplanes at the same time. Even after these events, the Federal Bureau of Investigation (FBI) and the Central Intelligence Agency (CIA) were receiving information that terrorists were planning to launch attacks within the United States. Then September 11 happened.

What made it possible for such attacks to happen on American soil? How is it that these acts of terrorism, which in some cases involved dozens of people around the world, could happen under the watch of the CIA, FBI, and local police? The answer lies, in part, in the freedoms of the American society.

If we follow the path of Mohammed Atta, the ringleader of the September 11 attacks, we can see how he took advantage of many American freedoms. In 2000, Atta attracted the attention of the CIA for his travels to Afghanistan, where he met Osama bin Laden, the founder of Al Qaeda. In June of that year, Atta entered the United States on a tourist visa. While the CIA monitors people only outside the United States, the FBI is responsible for monitoring people like Atta inside the country. It remains unclear whether the CIA informed the FBI about this dangerous man.

Once inside the United States, Atta was free to move about the country. He opened thirty-five bank accounts using false social security numbers, none of which was checked by any of the banks. In July 2000, he and another terrorist enrolled in a flight school in Florida to learn how to fly commercial airlines. He also received a partial license from the Federal Aviation Administration (FAA) in December. In less than a year, Mohammed Atta had gone from an individual under surveillance by the CIA to a licensed pilot in the United States.

In 2001, Mohammed Atta traveled between the United States and Europe at least four times. Immigration records indicate that on January 10, Atta arrived in Miami, Florida. Even though he had stayed longer than authorized on his previous visit, he was readmitted into the country. In May, he acquired a driver's license. He moved from place to place in Florida, signing multiple leases on apartments. He and his fellow terrorists acquired cell phones, credit cards, and mailboxes. But none of these companies could check his name in the CIA's computer system. At 5:53 AM on September 11, 2001, a video camera taped Atta through a security gate at Portland (Maine) International Jetport. The CIA, FBI, FAA, immigration services, flight schools, cell phone companies, credit card companies, and airport security had all had contact with him through surveillance, forms, and applications. Yet no one stopped him. Atta was simply a man traveling through the United States, enjoying the freedoms that millions of Americans take for granted. Three hours later, nearly 3,000 lives would be destroyed.

American president Thomas Jefferson once remarked that the price of freedom is eternal vigilance. Out of the wreckage of the September 11 terrorist attacks came a belief in the need for better vigilance. The 9/11 Commission report, which was released nearly three years after the attacks, stated:

> *Since the plotters were flexible and resourceful, we cannot know whether any single step or series of steps would have defeated them. What we can say with confidence is that none of the measures adopted by the U.S. government from 1998 to 2001 disturbed or even delayed the progress of the al Qaeda plot. Across the government, there were failures of imagination, policy, capabilities, and management.*

To protect Americans after September 11, better vigilance in the form of laws and better enforcement of them were required. One of the most important to appear was the Homeland Security Act of 2002.

CHAPTER ONE
Early Attempts at Homeland Security

While Mohammed Atta was freely boarding his flight, politicians in Washington were already trying to create new laws to improve the nation's ability to fight terrorism.

HART-RUDMAN COMMISSION

In 1998, the Defense Department created the U.S. Commission on National Security/21st Century (or the Hart-Rudman Commission, as it was more commonly known) to study the threat of terrorism. The commission issued a report eight months before September 11, 2001, recommending the formation of a National Homeland Security Agency. According to the report, the agency would be headed by a director who would be part of the president's cabinet. This director would have "responsibility for planning, coordinating, and integrating various U.S. government activities involved in homeland security." The commission proposed that the new agency would have control over the Border Patrol, Coast Guard, Customs Service, and other divisions of the FBI and Department of Commerce. Additionally, the new agency would manage the Federal Emergency Management Agency (FEMA), which is responsible for national emergency preparedness, including preparation for terrorist acts within the United States.

Gary Hart *(left)* and Warren Rudman, cochairmen of the U.S. Commission on National Security/21st Century, testify on national security issues before the House of Representatives Armed Service Committee on October 5, 1999. A little more than a year following this appearance, the commission issued a report calling for greater coordination between the federal agencies involved in national security.

According to Warren Rudman, cochair of the commission, the commission's report "had a very good response" from Congress.

President George W. Bush was not as supportive of the commission's findings. In an online article for *Slate* magazine, Jake Tapper reports that the president's aides indicated that he wanted FEMA to manage the nation's efforts against terrorism. The Hart-Rudman Commission and the president had different opinions on what part of the government should be responsible for domestic terrorism and whether that part of the government should be in the president's cabinet. These different opinions affected the bills that were later

Representative William Thornberry displays a newspaper headline about a plot to explode a dirty bomb in the United States during a June 2002 congressional hearing to combat terrorism. Thornberry was one of the leading advocates for the creation of a department of homeland security even before the September 11 attacks.

presented, and the threat of the president's veto made him a very important part of the process.

NATIONAL HOMELAND SECURITY AGENCY ACT (H.R. 1158)

Congress quickly added the recommendations of the Hart-Rudman Report to its agenda. Introduced in March 2001 by Representative William "Mac" Thornberry of Texas, the bill H.R. 1158 aimed to establish a National Homeland Security Agency, which would report to the National Security Council, a committee that is part of the executive branch. Accordingly, the new agency would be under the control of the president.

How a Bill Becomes a Law

Although the federal government creates hundreds of laws each year, the process of creating a single law can take a long time.

There are three branches of the federal government: legislative, executive, and judicial. The branch of the government that creates laws is the legislative branch, which is made up of the House of Representatives and the Senate. To create a new law, a bill (the proposed law) must be passed by the House and the Senate. It is then submitted to the president. If the president signs it, it becomes a law.

When a bill is first introduced in the House or Senate, it is given a number and title. The bill is then forwarded to the responsible committee, and the committee then debates the bill. It can change the bill, add amendments, or kill it, thereby removing it from discussion forever. If the committee approves the bill, it is introduced on the floor of the House or the Senate, where it will be debated by all of the representatives or senators, each of whom can introduce amendments or try to defeat the bill.

Consider a bill that originates in the House of Representatives. If the bill receives "yes" votes from more than half of the members of the House, it is passed to the Senate, where it goes directly to the floor for debate and a vote. The Senate can defeat the bill, pass it, or pass it with amendments. If the bill is passed with amendments, then a special committee made up of members of the House and the Senate irons out the differences between the two versions of the bill. The bill that this committee approves must then pass both chambers of Congress again.

A bill that passes both the Senate and House is submitted to the president, who can sign it into law or veto it. A vetoed bill is returned to the chamber where it originated for a new vote. If the bill receives two-thirds of all possible votes, it is passed to the other chamber, where it must receive another two-thirds vote. After that, the president's veto is overridden, and the bill becomes a law.

Although it's possible to override the veto with a two-thirds vote in both houses of Congress, an override does not often happen. To speed up the process of creating new laws, Congress must work with the president's staff and at times introduce legislation for him in Congress. As a result, the president has a great deal of influence on the bills in Congress.

Under the direction of the Federal Emergency Management Agency (FEMA), search and rescue workers from various federal, state, and local agencies sift through the rubble from the Oklahoma City bombing on April 21, 1995. FEMA is in charge of preparing for and cleaning up after major disasters, including natural events such as hurricanes and earthquakes; major accidents that threaten many lives; and terrorist strikes in the United States.

As the Hart-Rudman Commission recommended, the proposed National Homeland Security Agency would plan, coordinate, and bring together all government activities on homeland security. H.R. 1158 would transfer control of FEMA, the U.S. Customs Service, the Border Patrol, the Coast Guard, part of the FBI, and several other offices to the new agency. Also, under the proposed law, the director of the agency would be responsible for providing information from these agencies to the FBI and CIA.

The debate in Congress centered around several key questions: Was it a good idea to create this new office? Did it make sense to

President George W. Bush addresses the media at the swearing-in ceremony for Tom Ridge as assistant to the president on homeland security on October 8, 2001. In his remarks, Bush promised that Ridge would have "the full attention and complete support of the highest levels of our government."

organize this office under the National Security Council? Was it wise to have the Coast Guard report to this new agency? Legislators had different answers to these questions.

Because the president opposed putting FEMA under the control of an antiterrorism agency, there was little enthusiasm for H.R. 1158 in Congress. Like other antiterrorism bills before September 11, this bill never reached the floor of the House for debate.

AND THEN . . . A TERRIBLE WAKE-UP CALL

Six months after H.R. 1158 was introduced, 9/11 happened. While every presidential aide, representative, and senator agreed that something major had to be done, there was considerable disagreement on what to do.

Within a month of the attacks, President George W. Bush appointed Pennsylvania governor Tom Ridge to be his assistant on homeland security. In a press release announcing Ridge's appointment, he said:

> *The mission of the Office will be to develop and coordinate the implementation of a comprehensive national strategy to secure the United States from terrorist threats or attacks. The Office will coordinate the executive branch's efforts to detect, prepare for, prevent, protect against, respond to, and recover from terrorist attacks within the United States.*

According to the president, the new office was responsible for "a comprehensive national strategy," and he made it part of the executive branch. Many believed that the government needed a separate agency like the one proposed by H.R. 1158. Should the government's antiterrorist agency be under the control of the president (executive branch) or Congress (legislative branch)? This question would influence the antiterrorism bills that followed the terrorist attacks.

CHAPTER TWO

Crafting the Homeland Security Act of 2002

President Bush signed the Homeland Security Act of 2002 into law on November 25, more than a year after the terrorist attacks. Over the previous fourteen months, Congress had considered multiple bills on the same issue: how to create a powerful agency to prevent further terrorist attacks and to manage recovery from them. The struggle to consolidate the different bills proved to be a complex task.

S. 1534

One month after the September 11 attacks, Senator Joseph Lieberman of Connecticut introduced S. 1534. The bill was intended to create the National Office for Combating Terrorism inside the Office of the President. The director of this new office would be appointed by the president. However, like H.R. 1158, the bill also created a more powerful position, the cabinet-level secretary of national homeland security. The secretary would have a seat on the National Security Council and control of many federal agencies. Congress would have to approve the budget of the secretary of national homeland security, giving it greater influence over the antiterrorism organization. The director inside the president's office would be free to provide advice without having to worry about bosses in Congress.

The cabinet-level secretary, on the other hand, would receive funds to make changes, yet he or she would have to get that budget from Congress. Each position could be useful in different ways.

Sent to the Committee on Governmental Affairs, of which Lieberman was chairman, S. 1534 was the subject of eighteen hearings. During these hearings, the committee gathered information from many experts on terrorism as well as from other members of Congress. Senator Lieberman eventually concluded that "no single department could address all of the federal programs engaged in the war on terrorism." Accordingly, his committee chose not to forward the bill to the Senate floor. Lieberman and other members of Congress began working on broader legislation for the following year.

H.R. 4660 and S. 2452

In May 2002, Senator Lieberman and Congressman Mac Thornberry joined forces to introduce new bills in each chamber of Congress. H.R. 4660 had forty cosponsors, while S. 2452, Lieberman's companion bill in the Senate, had five cosponsoring senators who were willing to work to get the bill passed. By introducing these two bills at the same time in each house, the congressmen were hoping to speed the process of turning them into law. After each bill was amended in each house and then passed, the two Congressmen could lead a joint committee to iron out the differences between the two amended bills.

S. 2452 and H.R. 4660 called for the creation of the Department of Homeland Security (DHS), which would gain control over many federal agencies, such as the Coast Guard, the Border Patrol, and Customs Service, as well as the Department of Commerce and parts of other federal departments. The director of this proposed large department would have tremendous power and responsibility to protect the country. Both bills also required that the new director be given a seat on the National Security Council, so that this individual could be included among the key advisers to the president.

Senator Joe Lieberman was one of the leading congressional voices calling for the creation of a department of homeland security following the September 11 attacks. A former vice presidential candidate, he currently serves on four Senate committees: Homeland Security and Government Affairs, Armed Services, Environment, and Small Business.

Some of the reorganization plans in H.R. 1158 from the previous year had been softened to make them more acceptable in Congress and to the president. With broad support in Congress, these bills made progress toward becoming law. However, Congress had still not heard from Bush.

THE PRESIDENT ADDRESSES THE NATION

On June 6, 2002, the president advanced his official position. Speaking to the nation in a televised address, he said:

Tonight, I propose a permanent Cabinet-level Department of Homeland Security to unite essential agencies that must work more closely together: Among them, the Coast Guard, the Border Patrol, the Customs Service, Immigration officials, the Transportation Security Administration, and the Federal Emergency Management Agency.

While the president had originally rejected the recommendations of the Hart-Rudman Commission, the events of September 11 led him to agree with Congress. He now believed that a new, cabinet-level department, with control over major federal agencies that are responsible for detecting and stopping terrorists, was required.

Right after September 11, the nation had looked to President Bush for leadership and direction. To make the nation feel safer, he was expected to introduce the new law to protect the United States. Although S. 2452 and H.R. 4660 were already in Congress, many people felt that it was important for the country that a bill authorized by the president become the law that formed the new department.

H.R. 5005

The president's bill was delivered to the House of Representatives on June 18, 2002. Sponsored by Representative Dick Armey of Texas, H.R. 5005 represented the president's vision of the Department of Homeland Security.

H.R. 5005 was referred to thirteen house committees, including the House Select Committee on Homeland Security, which had been formed five days before. According to the rules of the new committee, any bill that sought to establish a Department of Homeland Security had to go through the committee. Because earlier House bills had been sent to other committees, they were no longer under consideration. H.R. 5005, the president's bill, would be used to form the new department.

Former House majority leader Dick Armey consults with Nancy Pelosi, the Democratic leader of the House of Representatives, as the Committee on Homeland Security begins debate on H.R. 5005.

CONGRESSIONAL BATTLES

H.R. 5005 landed in the House Select Committee with 118 cosponsors. With such broad support, the bill moved quickly through markup, the phase in which a bill is reviewed, edited, and rewritten by a committee. One month later, the amended bill was placed before the floor of the House. Over the next thirty-six hours, the entire House of Representatives debated the bill. Twenty-eight different amendments were presented, of which seventeen were successful. Late in the evening of July 26, H.R. 5005 passed in the House of Representatives by a vote of 295 in favor and 132 against.

Those Who Opposed H.R. 5005

After the long debates over H.R. 5005 and despite its many cosponsors, some in Congress still voted against it. One of these dissenters was Representative Anna Eshoo of California. According to her Web site, the congresswoman had significant concerns about this bill. She said, "Instead of increasing our safety on planes and in airports, the bill pushed back the deadline by a year for airports to screen all baggage."

Other members of Congress had different concerns about the bill and its amendments. After the compromise bill was finished in November, Senator Robert Byrd of West Virginia noted, "[The bill] had not been before any committee . . . There are 484 pages in this bill . . . If I were asked by the people of West Virginia, 'Senator Byrd, what is in that bill?' I could not answer." Senator Byrd also voted against the bill.

On July 30, H.R. 5005 was sent to the floor of the Senate. Over the next three months, the Senate piled on changes to the bill. There were amendments, and even amendments to the amendments. Many complained that the labor rights of the department's employees were not protected. There were strong opinions about whether the FBI and the CIA should be part of the new department. Amendments were added that seemed to have nothing to do with homeland security. The first anniversary of the September 11 attacks passed, and no new department had been formed.

Finally, on November 19, the Senate voted to invoke cloture. When a bill is on the floor of the Senate, each senator can speak for as long as he or she wants. In the past, senators used this right to prevent progress on a bill, even resorting to reading the phone book for hours. Such a move is called a filibuster. Cloture is the only way to prevent filibusters. If the Senate votes by two-thirds majority (or sixty-seven votes when all senators are in attendance) to invoke cloture, then total debate time on the matter is limited to thirty hours.

Later that day, an amended version of the bill was put to a vote in the Senate. It passed with ninety in favor, nine against, and one not voting. Since there had been amendments to H.R. 5005, the

President Bush signs the Homeland Security Act during a ceremony at the White House on November 25, 2002. The law ordered the most wide-ranging reorganization of the federal government in more than fifty years. The president described the law as a "historic action to defend the United States and protect our citizens against the dangers of a new era."

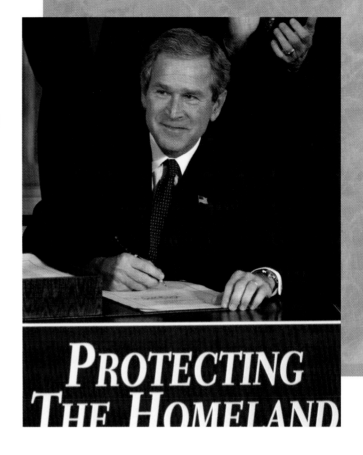

Senate bill had to go back to the House. Representative Armey asked for a unanimous vote from the House to approve the Senate's bill. That vote was achieved. The identical bill had passed both houses. President Bush signed H.R. 5005 into law on November 25.

CHAPTER THREE

The Department of Homeland Security

On January 24, 2003, the Department of Homeland Security began operations under the direction of Tom Ridge, who still maintained his other job in the President's Office of Homeland Security. The new department and the existing office began coordinating efforts to protect the United States from future terrorist attacks.

Beginning with a budget of $40 billion and 170,000 employees, the new department had plenty of resources. It had twenty-two agencies, many of which came from other departments. Most of these agencies are grouped into one of the four major subdivisions, called directorates, of the Department of Homeland Security. They are Border and Transportation Security, Emergency and Preparedness Response, Science and Technology, and Information Analysis and Infrastructure Protection. Each directorate has a specific set of responsibilities.

BORDER AND TRANSPORTATION SECURITY

The Border and Transportation Security group maintains the U.S. borders and protects transportation by air, sea, auto, and rail. The federal agencies that are now part of this group include the following:

Tom Ridge

On October 8, 2001, President Bush appointed Pennsylvania governor Tom Ridge to be the first homeland security adviser. For the next three years, Ridge led the nation's effort to detect, prevent, and recover from acts of terror on American soil.

Tom Ridge grew up in public housing and earned a scholarship to Harvard. He was drafted into the army while he was in law school and then earned a Bronze Star for valor while serving in Vietnam. He was elected to the U.S. Congress in 1982 and served for twelve years before becoming governor of Pennsylvania.

After H.R. 5005 was signed into law, Tom Ridge was appointed the first secretary of the Department of Homeland Security. He resigned from his position on November 30, 2004, and was replaced by Judge Michael Chertoff on February 15, 2005.

- **U.S. Customs Service.** This agency checks passports and now manages immigration, plant and animal inspection, and the entire U.S. Border Patrol. For the first time in history, all American borders are protected by one organization.
- **U.S. Citizenship and Immigration Services.** This new office decides who can immigrate to the United States and which immigrants can become citizens.
- **Federal Protective Service.** This service provides security at federal facilities.
- **Transportation Security Administration.** This agency provides security on public transportation, such as examining passengers and baggage at airports.
- **Federal Law Enforcement Training Center (FLETC).** FLETC trains federal security officers in emergency preparedness and counterterrorism techniques, including how to defuse bombs, handle hazardous materials, and search for terrorists.
- **Animal and Plant Health Inspection Service (APHIS).** APHIS is responsible for inspecting plants and animals at U.S. borders and across the country.

DHS ORGANIZATIONAL CHART

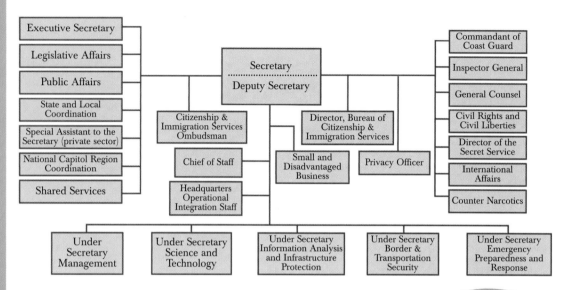

Executive Secretary

Legislative Affairs

Public Affairs

State and Local Coordination

Special Assistant to the Secretary (private sector)

National Capitol Region Coordination

Shared Services

Secretary
Deputy Secretary

Citizenship & Immigration Services Ombudsman

Chief of Staff

Headquarters Operational Integration Staff

Director, Bureau of Citizenship & Immigration Services

Small and Disadvantaged Business

Privacy Officer

Commandant of Coast Guard

Inspector General

General Counsel

Civil Rights and Civil Liberties

Director of the Secret Service

International Affairs

Counter Narcotics

Under Secretary Management

Under Secretary Science and Technology

Under Secretary Information Analysis and Infrastructure Protection

Under Secretary Border & Transportation Security

Under Secretary Emergency Preparedness and Response

This organizational chart for the Department of Homeland Security shows the department's major divisions as mandated by the Homeland Security Act of 2002. The accompanying seal features an American eagle, as well as a shield with images of the land, sea, and air. The shield also has twenty-two stars, representing the number of agencies that were combined into the Department of Homeland Security.

- **Office for Domestic Preparedness.** This new agency provides training, preparation, and equipment for responding to acts of terrorism within the United States. Its functions overlap with FEMA and other areas of the DHS.

EMERGENCY AND PREPAREDNESS RESPONSE

When a natural or man-made disaster strikes, this directorate directs the government's response to the event. It includes:

- **Federal Emergency Management Agency.** FEMA manages disasters, like hurricanes or acts of terrorism. It also develops the national emergency plan, which would be used to handle a terrorist attack.
- **Strategic National Stockpile and the National Disaster Medical System.** The national stockpile contains vital medical supplies for large disasters such as terrorist attacks. It is managed jointly by the DHS and the Department of Health and Human Services.
- **Nuclear Incident Response Team.** This organization provides personnel and special equipment to several federal agencies responsible for handling nuclear accidents and, if it happened, a nuclear weapon detonation.
- **Domestic Emergency Support Teams.** These teams from the Justice Department provide support services in the event of a domestic emergency.
- **National Domestic Preparedness Office (NDPO).** The NDPO coordinates federal agencies to assist state and local first responders, like policemen and firefighters, to train for handling weapons of mass destruction.

SCIENCE AND TECHNOLOGY

This directorate seeks to develop new science and better technology for detecting weapons of mass destruction and limiting their effects. It includes:

- **CBRN Countermeasures Programs.** These programs seek to promote technologies to detect and stop chemical, biological, radiological, and nuclear (CBRN) weapons.
- **Environmental Measurements Laboratory.** Working with the Department of Energy, the Environmental Measurements

Members of the Baltimore City Fire Department Hazmat Team participate in a mock terrorist attack in Baltimore, Maryland, on July 13, 2002. The emergency training exercise was put on by the University of Maryland Medical Center and the United States Air Force to simulate an attack including a weapon of mass destruction. Since its creation, the Department of Homeland Security has sponsored, coordinated, and monitored similar emergency drills.

Laboratory advances the science and technology of detecting and measuring nuclear events for the DHS.

- **National Bio-weapons Defense Analysis Center.** This agency of the Department of Defense examines how to better protect the United States against the threat of biological weapons.

- **Plum Island Animal Disease Center.** On Plum Island, New York, the Department of Agriculture researches how to protect the nation's animals from catching and spreading

Located 1.5 miles (2.4 kilometers) off the northeastern tip of Long Island, New York, the Plum Island Animal Disease Center is the only place in the United States where highly infectious animal diseases are studied. As such, it is a key agency in the Department of Homeland Security's mission to protect the United States from terrorist threats to the nation's agricultural resources.

diseases. If America's cows, pigs, and chickens were infected with a fatal disease, the national food supply would be at risk.

INFORMATION ANALYSIS AND INFRASTRUCTURE PROTECTION

This directorate gathers intelligence information from other agencies, such as the FBI and CIA, and analyzes it for threats to homeland security. Also, the directorate looks at the nation's roads, power supply, water supply, computer networks, and telephone networks to improve their protection. It includes:

- **Federal Computer Incident Response Center.** This office is charged with protecting the nation's Internet system from hackers and terrorists.

- **National Communications System.** The NCS is responsible for providing nationwide communications in the event of emergency or terrorist attack and for assisting in rebuilding the networks afterward.
- **National Infrastructure Protection Center.** The center focuses on how to better protect America's critical infrastructure, such as roads, water supply, telephone networks, and railroads.
- **Energy Security and Assurance Program.** This program provides protection for America's energy supply, including electrical, oil, and gas systems. If the nation's energy supply were attacked, the nation could be vulnerable to further attacks.

OTHER AGENCIES

Rounding out the twenty-two agencies that were consolidated under the Department of Homeland Security are the Secret Service and the U.S. Coast Guard. Their duties are as follow:

- **Secret Service.** The Secret Service protects the president, the vice president, their families, and visiting foreign leaders.
- **Coast Guard.** The U.S. Coast Guard secures the coasts of the United States. It stops smugglers, secures ports, rescues stranded boaters, inspects foreign vessels, and enforces the laws of the sea.

THE LARGEST GOVERNMENTAL REORGANIZATION IN FIFTY YEARS

The first job of the DHS is to prevent future terrorist attacks in the United States, and that task is enormous. As Dr. Pietro Nivola, a scholar at the Brookings Institute in Washington, D.C., said, "One of the grave difficulties with Homeland Security is the number of imaginable targets—we're a country of 3 million square miles [7,769,964 sq. km], 75 huge population centers and thousands of miles of coastline."

Additionally, millions of peaceful people enter the country each year at the borders, ports, and airports. More than six million shipping containers arrive on boats each year. And everyone in the United States needs water and food, supplies that could be contaminated or poisoned. It's impossible to guard against all possible targets.

How could the secretary of homeland security organize so many people in so many different offices, who have been working for different organizations for years? For example, the Office for Domestic Preparedness, formerly part of the Department of Justice, and the National Domestic Preparedness Office, formerly part of the FBI, had each been responsible for preparing the country for a terrorist attack. Now, these two offices were under the new department. Was one of them unnecessary? If not, how were they going to work together? And how were other organizations going to decide with which office to work?

The above example is just one of thousands of problems that had to be resolved in the largest reorganization of government in fifty years. To keep the United States safe, the Department of Homeland Security must work with local police, water officials, and port authorities, who are expected to be the eyes and ears of homeland security. Coordinating all of these outside organizations creates problems, too. On March 1, 2003, the Department of Homeland Security assumed control of these twenty-two agencies and began to address these problems.

CHAPTER FOUR

Homeland Security Now and in the Future

The Department of Homeland Security employs more than 180,000 people dedicated to watching over the United States. The price of eternal vigilance is now more than $40 billion a year. Is the Department of Homeland Security doing a good job?

Several years have passed since the September 11 attacks, and no major act of terrorism has occurred in the United States. Around the world, though, Americans have been kidnapped, assassinated, and bombed. Groups such as Al Qaeda still want to cause havoc in the United States, and terrorism still ranks as one of the top concerns for Americans.

While the federal government has worked hard to prevent another terrorist attack on American soil, progress in making changes in the Department of Homeland Security continues at a slow pace. Representative Thornberry noted this in a December 2003 interview.

Certain people [in the DHS] still have the same uniforms and go to work at the same places and have the same computer databases and, I'm told, continue to have separate rules and regulations for how they conduct their work . . . What I can't forget, in my impatience, is they also have a job to do everyday. There are folks on the border with guns on their hips,

The Patriot Act

On October 26, 2001, President Bush signed the Patriot Act into law. A companion law to the Homeland Security Act, it extended the powers of law enforcement officials to gather information about suspected terrorists. Among other things, it allows for wiretapping public phones, spying on public computers, and loosening the requirements for putting Americans under surveillance.

Many people believe that the Patriot Act violates individuals' right to privacy. For example, the federal government can force libraries to provide information on the books that individuals have checked out. Should the government have this right?

Opponents have argued that the protection of individual rights is one of the most important functions of the constitution. Supporters of the Patriot Act, however, argue that the need to stop terrorists before they can act is more important than this intrusion into private lives.

and they guard the border every day. And so you can't completely take them out of their job to work your organizational magic on them.

Thornberry presents a good example. To meet the goals of H.R. 5005, border guards needed additional training in how to detect terrorists and their weapons. However, the guards still had jobs to do at the border every day; only a few of them could get trained at a time. Similar slow movement was seen in other areas of the DHS.

HOMELAND SECURITY AND THE BILL OF RIGHTS

In broadening the powers of the federal government to gather information about individuals in America, the new Department of Homeland Security has created concerns that civil rights have been violated. Some believe that Muslim groups have already been unfairly targeted in ways that other groups are not. For example, the American Civil Liberties Union (ACLU) has filed a lawsuit on behalf of Americans who have been incorrectly placed on the nationwide no-fly list. Balancing homeland security and civil rights may be a very difficult issue to resolve.

A lawyer for the American Civil Liberties Union (ACLU) of North California announces on April 2003 plans to sue the federal government on behalf of people who have been incorrectly placed on the no-fly list. Two people whose names appeared on the list look on. Organizations such as the ACLU, as well as many members of Congress, are concerned that many American freedoms are unnecessarily being sacrificed in homeland security legislations.

THE 9/11 COMMISSION

In late 2002, President Bush formed the 9/11 Commission to research why and how the September 11 attacks occurred. Based on eighteen months of interviews and research, the 9/11 Commission released its final report on July 22, 2004. Its Executive Summary contained several ideas to bring together the counterterrorism efforts in the federal government and to improve the sharing of information about terrorists. The president thanked

Michael Chertoff addresses
Department of Homeland Security
employees after being sworn in as
the department's secretary on
February 16, 2005. Prior to his
appointment, he served as a
United States Court of Appeals
judge. He is a former lawyer,
federal prosecutor, and assistant
U.S. attorney general.

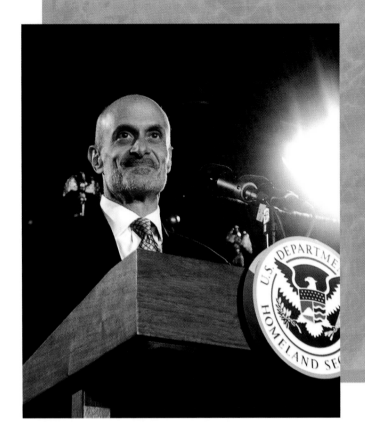

the 9/11 Commission for its efforts and agreed with many of its
findings. He said:

> *We are already implementing the vast majority of those recommendations that can be enacted without a vote of Congress . . . Congress needs to create the position of the National Intelligence Director and take other measure to make our intelligence community more effective. These reforms are necessary to stay ahead of the threats. I urge Congress to act quickly, so I can sign them into law.*

In October, the House of Representatives passed the 9/11
Commission Implementation Act (H.R. 10) by a vote of 282 to 134.
Among its sections, H.R. 10 included the following actions, which
were recommended by the 9/11 Commission report:

- **A new national intelligence director.** As the 9/11 Commission and President Bush recommended, this new office would be in the Office of the President and appointed by the president. This director would have a budget and the right to set policies and share information across the intelligence community.
- **The Faster and Smarter Funding for First Responders Act (H.R. 3266).** This separate act makes it easier to quickly provide funding to fire departments and police forces, which are likely to be the first groups to respond to a terrorist attack. The 9/11 Commission report said that these groups were not getting funds fast enough to improve preparation for the next terrorist attack.
- **A better training program for border guards.** As Representative Thornberry noted, retraining of border guards was slow. By increasing their training and improving the sharing of intelligence, guards at America's borders will be better prepared to capture terrorists.
- **Blocking terrorist travel and funding.** In addition to better guard training, H.R. 10 recommended improving the security of travel documents, like passports and entry visas. With improved security, these documents would be harder to forge. Also, H.R. 10 suggested steps to cut down terrorists' access to funds.

H.R. 10 passed shortly before the close of the 108th session of Congress and the 2004 presidential election. After President Bush's reelection, H.R. 10 was combined with a similar Senate bill (S. 2845) to become the National Intelligence Reform Act of 2004. President Bush signed it into law on December 17, 2004. Among other measures, the law created a national counterterrorism center and an independent board to review civil liberties issues related to the ongoing fight to reduce the threat of terrorism in the United States.

The 9/11 Commission (officially the National Commission on Terrorist Attacks upon the United States) was formed by President Bush after intense pressure from family members of victims of the terrorist attacks. The ten-member commission is pictured here on June 16, 2004, one day before it held its final public hearing. The commission found that the nation was safer than it was before September 11, 2001, but not safe.

THE TRUE TEST OF HOMELAND SECURITY

The true test of the Department of Homeland Security is time. Fifty years in the future, will the history of the DHS be successful or not? As President Bush said in a July 2004 speech, "Terrorists only need to be right once; we need to be right every single time." In protecting the American homeland, the DHS has an extremely difficult job.

However, the responsibility for a secure America is not just the job of the DHS. As the great American lawyer Clarence Darrow said, "You can protect your liberties in this world only by protecting the other man's freedom. You can be free only if I am free." Like Darrow, many Americans believe that in a world in which nations are becoming more connected, citizens of the United States cannot be free unless citizens of other countries are also free.

In places like Afghanistan and Iraq, the U.S. military has over-thrown governments that did not allow citizens to be free. Some people in those countries, however, do not believe in the American ideas of freedom. In the fight to free those countries, thousands of people have died. Some have argued that the death and bloodshed have only made people more angry at the United States. Some of these people may become terrorists willing to sacrifice their lives to kill Americans, just like Mohammed Atta did.

However, many people still look to the United States as a sign of freedom and opportunity. From beyond the golden door at the Statue of Liberty, American citizens can protect the homeland by welcoming visitors. While the cost of protecting the ideals of free-dom and opportunity continues to rise, by holding on to them we may one day achieve the greatest ideal of all: worldwide peace.

GLOSSARY

act A bill that passes in both the House and the Senate. An act that is signed by the president becomes a law.

amendment A motion to change part of the text of a bill or another amendment. Amendments to the bill are called first-degree amendments. Amendments to amendments are called second degree.

bill A proposal in Congress to create or change a law. If a bill passes both the House and Senate, it is passed to the president for his signature, after which it becomes law. Bills introduced in the House are labeled "H.R." followed by a unique number. The names of Senate bills begin with "S."

budget The amount of money that a company or organization has allocated to spend on its programs.

cabinet A collection of presidential advisers who run the departments of the federal government. The cabinet meets frequently with the president to advise him on government policy.

CIA The Central Intelligence Agency is responsible for gathering information about individuals, organizations, or national governments in other countries that may be a threat to the interests of the United States.

cloture The process by which a debate or filibuster can be ended in the Senate. When invoked, cloture limits additional debate on a bill to thirty total hours. Cloture requires the votes of 60 percent of the Senate.

companion bill When a bill is introduced in the Senate, a similar or identical bill can be introduced in the House to speed the process of turning the bill into law. A companion bill to a House bill can also be introduced in the Senate.

Congress The legislative branch of the federal government. It includes the House of Representatives and the Senate.

cosponsor In either chamber of Congress, a member who lends support and adds his or her name to a bill sponsored by another member.

executive branch The Office of the President of the United States and all supporting administration, including the cabinet.

FAA The Federal Aviation Administration is responsible for controlling licensing of pilots and American airspace.

FBI The Federal Bureau of Investigation is responsible for enforcing federal law in America, including the capture of terrorists.

federal Of or pertaining to a form of government in which the central government is separate from the government of its states. The U.S. government is federal in form.

filibuster According to the rules of Congress, a member can speak on the floor of either chamber of Congress for as long as he or she desires. To prevent progress or votes on legislation, some congressmen have continued to speak, refusing to yield their time to another. Such action, called a filibuster, has prevented bills from passing.

House The House of Representatives, consisting of 435 members from all parts of the United States. Each state is represented by a number of representatives in Washington, D.C., based on the population of the state. As the most populated state in the nation, California has the most members in the House of Representatives.

immigration The act of moving into one country from another.

intelligence Information collected by the government about other nations.

joint resolutions Resolutions that are passed in both the House and Senate to make constitutional amendments or to fix technical errors in other legislation.

judicial branch The branch of the federal government responsible for interpreting the law. Its highest authority is the United States Supreme Court.

kill When a bill has been stalled in a committee or voted down permanently, it is said to be killed. Although no further action can be taken on a killed bill, a new bill containing the same language as the original bill can be introduced in Congress.

law A bill that has passed both the House and the Senate and has been signed by the president of the United States.

legislative branch The branch of the federal government responsible for creating laws. In Washington, it is composed of two bodies: the House and the Senate.

legislator Anyone who is responsible for creating law. Members of Congress are legislators.

markup The process through which a law is debated, changed, and rewritten by committees and subcommittees in the House or Senate before it is sent to the floor of either chamber.

override When the president vetoes a bill, Congress can override the veto and turn the bill into law by a second vote in each chamber of Congress. If all members of Congress vote, 290 House votes and 67 Senate votes must be in favor of the bill.

section One part of a congressional bill.

Senate The more powerful chamber of Congress, composed of two elected members from each state, for a total of 100 members.

sponsor The legislator who leads the effort to get a bill passed in Congress.

veto To reject a piece of legislation, preventing it from becoming law.

FOR MORE INFORMATION

Department of Homeland Security
Washington, DC 20528
(202) 282-8000
Web site: http://www.dhs.gov

Office of Homeland Security
The White House
1600 Pennsylvania Avenue NW
Washington, DC 20500
(202) 456-1414
Web site: http://www.whitehouse.gov/homeland

Web Sites

Due to the changing nature of Internet links, the Rosen Publishing Group, Inc., has developed an online list of Web sites related to the subject of this book. This site is updated regularly. Please use this link to access the list:

http://www.rosenlinks.com/lallp/hosa

FOR FURTHER READING

Campbell, Geoffrey A. *A Vulnerable America: An Overview of National Security* (Library of Homeland Security). San Diego, CA: Lucent Books, 2003.

Corona, Laurel. *Hunting Down the Terrorists: Declaring War and Policing Global Violations* (Library of Homeland Security). San Diego, CA: Lucent Books, 2003.

Gottfried, Ted. *Homeland Security Versus Constitutional Rights.* Brookfield, CT: Twenty-First Century Books, 2003.

Kerrigan, Michael. *Department of Homeland Security* (Rescue and Prevention Defending Our Nation). Broomall, PA: Mason Crest Publishers, 2003.

Sanna, Ellyn. *Homeland Security Officer* (Careers with Character). Broomall, PA: Mason Crest Publishers, 2003.

Schaffer, Donna, and Alfred Meyer. *Secretary of Homeland Security* (America's Leaders). San Diego, CA: Blackbirch Press, 2003.

Stewart, Gail B. *Defending the Borders: The Role of Border and Immigration Control* (Library of Homeland Security). San Diego, CA: Lucent Books, 2003.

Torr, James D. *Responding to Attack: Firefighters and Police* (Library of Homeland Security). San Diego, CA: Lucent Books, 2003.

BIBLIOGRAPHY

Center for Cooperative Research. "Complete 911 Timeline." Retrieved October 1, 2004 (http://www.cooperativeresearch.org/timeline.jsp?timeline=complete_911_timeline&timeperiod=0:10am-11:50pm%2011%20Sept%202001).

C-SPAN. "C-SPAN Congressional Glossary." Retrieved October 19, 2004 (http://www.c-span.org/guide/congress/glossary/alphalist.htm).

C-SPAN. "Department of Homeland Security Reorganization." 2004. Retrieved October 26, 2004 (http://www.c-span.org/homelandsecurity/chart.asp).

Federation for American Immigration Reform. "U.S. Immigration History." July 2004. Retrieved September 24, 2004 (http://www.fairus.org/Research/Research.cfm?ID=1820&c=2).

Freedom Files. "Homeland Security." 2003. Retrieved October 18, 2004 (http://www.freedomfiles.org/war/homeland.htm).

Global Security Newswire. "US Responses: New Bill Would Create Cabinet-Level Homeland Security Position." May 3, 2002. Retrieved October 20, 2004 (http://www.nti.org/d_newswire/issues/thisweek/2002_5_3_terr.html).

Gottfried, Ted. *Homeland Security Versus Constitutional Rights.* Brookfield, CT: Twenty-First Century Books, 2003.

GOV.com. "Department of Homeland Security." 2003. Retrieved October 26, 2004 (http://www.gov.com/agency/dhs).

Henry, Kate. Government Security. "Can Tom Ridge Make a Difference?" April 9, 2002. Retrieved October 22, 2004 (http://govtsecurity.securitysolutions.com/ar/security_tom_ridge_difference).

House of Representatives. "Congressional Record H8596." November 13, 2002. Retrieved October 21, 2004 (http://thomas.loc.gov).

House of Representatives. "Congressional Record H9040-9114." November 22, 2002. Retrieved October 21, 2004 (http://thomas.loc.gov).

House of Representatives. "Congresswoman Anna Eschoo: Homeland Security." Retrieved October 22, 2004 (http://eshoo.house.gov/legislative/homeland.aspx).

House of Representatives. "Representative Offices." Retrieved October 18, 2004 (http://www.house.gov/house/ MemberWWW.shtml).

House of Representatives. "The Subcommittee on Economic Development, Public Buildings, & Emergency Management: Hearing on Combating Terrorism: Options to Improve the Federal Response." April 21, 2001. Retrieved October 19, 2004 (http://www.house.gov/transportation/pbed/04-24-01/ 04-24-01memo.html).

House of Representatives. "Thornberry, Lieberman Mount Bipartisan, Bicameral Push for Homeland Security Reorganization." May 2, 2002. Retrieved October 20, 2004 (http://www.house.gov/thornberry/news_releases/2002/ May2200202.htm).

House of Representatives Rules Committee. "Summary of Amendments Submitted to the Rules Committee on H.R. 5005, Homeland Security Act of 2002." July 25, 2002. Retrieved October 20, 2004 (http://www.house.gov/rules/ sum_homeland_107.htm).

House of Representatives Select Committee on Homeland Security. "Chairman Cox Hails Passage Of 9-11 Commission Reforms." October 8, 2004. Retrieved October 30, 2004 (http://hsc. house.gov/release.cfm?id=263).

House Republican Conference. "Thornberry Welcomes Lieberman Proposal to Establish National Homeland Security Agency." October 11, 2001. Retrieved October 20, 2004 (http://www. gop.gov/item-news.asp?docId=52970).

Infoplease. "How a Bill Becomes a Law." Retrieved October 16, 2004 (http://www.infoplease.com/ipa/A0101183.html).

Jones, Alison, Stephanie Pickering, and Megan Thomson, eds. *Dictionary of Quotations.* New York, NY: Chambers, 1997.

Morgan, Curtis, David Kidwell, and Oscar Corral. "Prelude to Terror." *Miami Herald,* September 22, 2001. Retrieved October 1, 2004 (http://web.archive.org/web/20011110021626/ www.miami.com/herald/special/news/worldtrade/digdocs/ 000518.htm).

National Commission on Terrorist Attacks upon the United States. "The 9-11 Report: Executive Summary." July 22, 2004. Retrieved October 27, 2004 (http://www.9-11commission.gov/ report/911Report_Exec.pdf).

Navy League. "Mac Thornberry: Congressional Agent for Change." December 2003. Retrieved October 20, 2004 (http://www. navyleague.org/sea_power/dec_03_17.php).

Office of Legislative Policy and Analysis. "Legislative Updates: 107th Congress." Retrieved October 20, 2004 (http://olpa.od.nih.gov/legislation/107/pendinglegislation/ homelandsecurity. asp).

Polling Report. "Problems and Priorities." October 21, 2004. Retrieved October 27, 2004 (http://www.pollingreport.com/ prioriti.htm).

Safire, William. "You Are a Suspect." *New York Times,* November 14, 2002. Retrieved October 21, 2004 (http://www.nytimes.com/ 2002/11/14/opinion/14SAFI.html).

Tapper, Jake. Salon Media Group. "'We Predicted It.'" September 12, 2001. Retrieved October 18, 2004 (http://www.salon.com/ politics/feature/2001/09/12/bush).

Truthout. "Truthout Address: The Homeland Security Act of 2002." November 14, 2002. Retrieved October 20, 2004 (http://www. truthout.com/docs_02/11.20A.byrd.home.htm).

U.S. Department of State. "Significant Terrorist Incidents, 1961–2003: A Brief Chronology." March 2004. Retrieved October 18, 2004 (http://www.state.gov/r/pa/ho/pubs/fs/index.cfm?docid=5902).

The White House. "Biography of Secretary Tom Ridge." October 8, 2001. Retrieved October 19, 2004 (http://www.whitehouse.gov/homeland/ridgebio.html).

The White House. "Department of Homeland Security." Retrieved October 20, 2004 (http://www.whitehouse.gov/homeland).

The White House. "President Bush Discusses Progress in Homeland Security in Illinois." July 22, 2004. Retrieved October 27, 2004 (http://www.whitehouse.gov/news/releases/2004/07/20040722-12.html).

The White House. "President Establishes Office of Homeland Security." October 11, 2001. Retrieved October 25, 2004 (http://www.whitehouse.gov/news/releases/2001/10/20011008.html).

The White House. "President's Remarks on Homeland Security in New Jersey." October 18, 2004. Retrieved October 20, 2004 (http://www.whitehouse.gov/news/releases/2004/10/20041018-11.html).

The White House. "Remarks by the President in Address to the Nation." June 6, 2002. Retrieved October 19, 2004 (http://www.whitehouse.gov/news/releases/2002/06/20020606-8.html).

Wikipedia. "Department of Homeland Security." October 17, 2004. Retrieved October 22, 2004 (http://en.wikipedia.org/wiki/United_States_Department_of_Homeland_Security).

Wikipedia. "Mohammed Atta." September 23, 2004. Retrieved October 1, 2004 (http://en.wikipedia.org/wiki/Mohammed_Atta).

INDEX

About the Author

Steven P. Olson is a writer and researcher who has written many books for young adults. Like many Americans, he became deeply interested in how the United States was going to protect itself from terrorist attacks after 9/11. He closely followed the development of the Department of Homeland Security, as well as the various congressional debates and legislations regarding counterterrorism. He lives in Oakland, California.

Photo Credits

Cover © Royalty-Free/Corbis; pp. 5, 9, 10, 12, 17, 19, 24, 26, 32, 35 © AP/Wide World Photos; p. 13 © Ron Sachs/Corbis; p. 21 © Reuters/Corbis; p. 27 © Henny Ray Abrams/Reuters/Corbis; p. 33 © Micah Walter/Reuters/Corbis.

Designer: Thomas Forget; Editor: Wayne Anderson